PIECES

INTO

PLACE

PIECES
INTO
PLACE

A Story of Faith, Prayer, and
God's Ultimate Plan for a Family

Kimberlee Koehn

*A*zure *S*eas
PUBLISHING

Pieces into Place: A Story of Faith, Prayer, and God's Ultimate Plan for a Family

All Scripture quotations, unless otherwise indicated, are taken from the Holy Bible, New International Version®, NIV®. Copyright ©1973, 1978, 1984, 2011 by Biblica, Inc.™ Used by permission of Zondervan. All rights reserved worldwide. www.zondervan.com. The "NIV" and "New International Version" are trademarks registered in the United States Patent and Trademark Office by Biblica, Inc.™

Scripture quotations marked (CEV) are from the Contemporary English Version Copyright © 1991, 1992, 1995 by American Bible Society, Used by Permission.

Scripture quotations marked NLT are taken from the Holy Bible, New Living Translation, copyright ©1996, 2004, 2007, 2013, 2015 by Tyndale House Foundation. Used by permission of Tyndale House Publishers, Inc., Carol Stream, Illinois 60188. All rights reserved.

Scripture quotations marked ESV are from The ESV® Bible (The Holy Bible, English Standard Version®), copyright © 2001 by Crossway, a publishing ministry of Good News Publishers. Used by permission. All rights reserved.

Scripture quotations from The Authorized (King James) Version. Rights in the Authorized Version in the United Kingdom are vested in the Crown. Reproduced by permission of the Crown's patentee, Cambridge University Press.

Scripture taken from *THE MESSAGE*. Copyright © 1993, 1994, 1995, 1996, 2000, 2001, 2002. Used by permission of NavPress Publishing Group.

Cover photograph courtesy of Pexels.com

ISBN 978-1-950058-06-8

www.azureseaspublishing.com

Azure Seas
PUBLISHING

TABLE OF CONTENTS

EXIT PIECE

"For I know the plans I have for you," declares the LORD, "plans to prosper you and not harm you, plans to give you hope and a future."

— Jeremiah 29:11

On January 21, 2020, the first confirmed case of the coronavirus in the United States was announced in Everett, Washington.

On January 22, 2020, twin boys were born in Guangzhou, China.

On January 30, the World Health Organization declared a global health emergency.

And on January 31, the United States issued a nationwide travel ban from China—for non-US citizens.

The twin boys, Jeremy and Jonathan Perrone, were US citizens. And their parents, Matt and Ellen Perrone, watched anxiously during Ellen's third trimester as COVID-19 evolved into a global crisis.

Once the babies were born, the doctors recommended waiting eight weeks before air travel. So Matt, Ellen, Jeremy, Jonathan, and Matt's mom, Karen, who had flown in a few weeks before the births, waited. Their nights were sleepless with the normal stresses and anxieties associated with newborns and with the entirely abnormal circumstances related to COVID-19, which was sending the entire world into chaos and panic.

On March 3, 2020, eight days before the World Health Organization (WHO) declared COVID-19 a global pandemic, Matt, Ellen, Karen, Jeremy, and Jonathan Perrone went running through the Shenyang Taoxian International Airport, desperate to make one of the last flights leaving China for the United States before the lockdown took effect. Ellen was still nursing, Karen was limping, unaware she had a torn meniscus, and Matt had just recovered from food poisoning, terrified lingering symptoms would be misinterpreted as COVID-19.

As the call for boarding blared over the intercom, security stopped them, refusing to let them pass. They looked at each other, panicking, and then they heard, "Last call!"

PRESS PAUSE

I'd be remiss to tell you that that moment—the airport moment—is THE MOMENT.

Sure, it is a moment. It is a big moment. Like many moments in our lives, it might have seemed like the biggest moment for Matt and Ellen as it was happening. I don't want to belittle that. But that moment is not why I'm telling you this story. That moment is not why you're holding this book in your hands. That moment is a culmination of little moments—of millions upon millions of perfect pieces that fell into place in God's perfect timing.

When I sat down to hear Matt and Ellen's story, I felt my own faith swell. For it spelled out, clear as day, that God's hand had been on their lives from the moment they were born. He gave purpose to each step they took, even those that weren't easy. He had a plan for each of their lives, not only as individuals, but as a couple. He wrote their story piece by piece to create a tangible testament to his faithfulness, and not only for their sake.

As I spoke with Matt and Ellen, it didn't take long for me to realize that their story was part of my purpose, and part of God's plan for my life. Perhaps it is part of yours too.

Maybe God thought of me when he started to weave together Matt and Ellen's story, knowing they'd need someone to help them tell it, and so he put people in my life that encouraged me to write from an early age. Maybe God thought of you as Matt and Ellen ran through the airport, knowing you'd find restorative faith in their story. Maybe God is thinking of someone else as you read these words, knowing exactly how you will use that faith to change their life, and how it will all ripple outward, furthering His plans for good.

Maybe, I wondered to myself, as I heard Matt and Ellen's story.

The more I listened, the more that maybe became a definitely, an obviously, an abundant and overwhelming YES!

That is why I am telling you this story.

That is the moment. The moment when we not only see that God is at work, but that He has always been working, and that He will always keep working in our lives. We don't always notice His hand or even His influence when we look at the surface of our own lives, but when we hear stories like Matt and Ellen's, we are given better tools to dig deeper in our search for Him—both in our future and in our past.

In *God Built*, Matt Farrar wrote, "When we look backward, we see that God was in control even when it looked like our lives were out of control."

So let's look backward. Let's see where this story started and watch it unfold just as God planned, remembering that God's faithfulness exists for all of us, every day, even when we don't recognize it right away.

For Jesus said, "My Father is always working, and so am I" (John 5:17 NLT).

THE STORY BEGINS

"Perhaps you were born for such a time as this."

— *Esther 4:14*

Matt

Matthew "Matt" Perrone was born April 8, 1992, in Sylmar, California. He was the third of four children to John and Karen Perrone, with an older sister, and both an older and younger brother.

Matt was a good kid. He was quiet, caring, and diligent and his family was tight-knit. They played board games and watched movies together, had family dinners and delighted in each other's company, and on the weekends they went to church.

When Matt was little, he liked to cook alongside his mom. He would stand beside her, watching her mix and season and create, and fell in love with food. It became his first passion and gave wings to his first dream. As he stirred, broiled, baked, and fried, he dreamed of becoming a chef, of opening his own restaurant—maybe Italian or Mexican food, or a unique fusion of both. He liked that his food could speak for him. That he could give it as a gift for his family to enjoy. He liked that he could express himself in flavors and combinations.

In school, Matt loved math and science and never missed an assignment, determined to get good grades. He was shy and soft spoken, never one to raise his hand or draw attention to himself. He had a small group of close friends that he'd known since kindergarten and got involved in his local youth group early on.

Coming from a Christian family, Matt was taught to trust in God's plan from a young age. As a result, he often didn't look too far forward or worry about the future. He took things step by step, moving slowly and quietly through each day as it came.

Ellen

Ellen Perrone (she asked not to use her maiden name) has two birthdays.

Technically, she was born in November 1993 in southeast Guangdong, China (about 100 miles east of Hong Kong). Like her siblings, Ellen was born at home rather than a hospital, so she wasn't given a birth certificate. Ellen's parents marked her birthday as March 15, 1993—primarily so she could begin her education sooner.

Ellen is the fourth of five children, which remains very uncommon—not to mention a fine-able offense—in China since 1979.[1]

Ellen's oldest sibling, a brother, was the pride and joy of her parents and grandparents. He was spoiled and cherished, considered a dream come true—as many sons are in Chinese society.

A 2011 article for *The Guardian* noted that since daughters "marry out" of their family, thus offering their parents no value after marriage, having a girl has often been seen as "wasteful." Meanwhile sons, who carry on the family bloodline and are historically capable of tougher work, and thus better earnings, are viewed as a parent's "pension."[2]

With this in mind, soon after Ellen's eldest brother was born, her parents got pregnant again, hopeful for a second boy to complete their family.

Ellen's brother was born in 1988, almost a decade after the One Child Policy took effect in China. Thus, her parents' plans to have even one more child violated this policy. However, Ellen's grandfather worked for the regional government's family planning division. His job was to enforce the fine placed on families that had more than one child, putting him in a position of power and allowing him to wave the fee for his own family. He encouraged Ellen's parents to have another child—namely another son. This, however, would not be the case. They had three girls in a row, the third of whom was Ellen.

After Ellen was born, her family planned to put her up for adoption. With little to no use for so many girls, and the unrelenting pressure her grandparents put on her parents to have another son, they simply wanted to give her away and try again.

But then Ellen's grandmother had a vision—a sign from somewhere beyond. She told Ellen's parents she saw Ellen holding the hand of a young boy—a second son—and in order to make that vision come true, they would need to keep Ellen.

So they did.

And a year later, Ellen's younger brother was born.

Matt

By design, Matt is most similar to his dad, John. Not only are they like-minded in spirit and bonded by similar interests, but they walk and talk almost identically. Oftentimes growing up, Matt would answer the home phone and have to interrupt friends and family as they ran into a story or question under the assumption they were talking to his dad.

John often took Matt to church workdays, teaching him how to make repairs and run electrical wiring, which gave him an appreciation for technology and a curiosity that began to blossom.

At a computer repair shop owned by a family friend, Matt liked to hang out and watch the pieces be taken apart and then put back together. The process fascinated him. Occasionally, he would help out, playing apprentice the way he did with his dad, absorbing everything he could. One day, the friend told Matt, who was in middle school at the time, that he would give him a computer, or, more specifically, all the *parts* of a computer, and if Matt could put it together himself, he could keep it.

When Matt agreed, an entirely new world opened up for him. He began to dream of creating special effects for action movies. He imagined himself wearing a headset that kept him up to date on the latest national threat as he did everything he could to set up and protect the defense systems keeping his country safe.

At the same time, Matt began going on mission trips with his church youth group, going to places like Mexico and the Dominican Republic, to serve people and communities in need and introduce them to Jesus.

On one particular trip, as the sun shone high in the sky, Matt sat down on the porch steps of a newly built house his group was painting and looked out at the city. It was a place wholly unfamiliar to him, filled with people living different lives with different traditions, different cultures, and different dreams.

He took a moment to pray, to talk to God about this place, and in doing so, he began to feel a stirring in his heart. As he continued to look around, he suddenly felt a newfound familiarity of sorts. Matt felt God speak to him, "Someday you're going to live in a place like this."

Matt was surprised. Curious. Confused. He took a good look around, searching for answers. At second glance, he began to notice the pink and green color palette that defined the city. He noticed the people walking from place to place rather than driving, and the otherworldliness of the city compared to the smog and skyscrapers found back home in Southern California. But nothing he saw looked like an answer.

What do you mean? He asked God.

Will I live here?

Will it be for missionary work?

Or will I just make an international move?

And to where?

For what reason?

There was no answer.

Matt stood up and got back to work, his imagination running wild. For the rest of the trip, his daydreams took him all over the world, and in and out of hundreds of different lives, though none of those daydreams would come close to what God had in store.

Ellen

Remember how Ellen has two birthdays? Well, being both a middle child and the third youngest daughter, Ellen's family paid very little attention to her. Even with two dates to choose from, her family never celebrated her birthday.

The neighbors next door, however, always did. That couple, whom she called her aunt and uncle—a very common moniker in China for adults, even if you bear no relation—had three girls and one boy.

Unlike Ellen's family, the couple did not view having three daughters in a negative light, and treated Ellen as one of their own. Their son, Chris, was born one day before Ellen, so they always invited her over to celebrate the two of them on the same day.

In spending time with them, Ellen came to learn that they were Christians. By comparison, her family, like many in China, was Buddhist, and while Christianity was not unheard of, it was extremely frowned upon in her hometown. In some parts of China, pronouncing their Christian faith could have had the family cast out or punished, but, as a kung fu master and Chinese medicine doctor, her uncle was well respected in the community and was met with no backlash for his outward religious beliefs.

As a result, Ellen was given a safe space to learn about Jesus and she started attending church with them regularly.

Matt

After graduating high school, Matt was accepted to California Lutheran University in Thousand Oaks, California (about 40 miles from his hometown), to pursue a degree in computer science. Shortly after completing his first year however, Matt was diagnosed with gastroesophageal reflux disease (GERD). Typically, this is caused by a dysfunctional valve at the top of the stomach and bottom of the esophagus, but in Matt's case it was the lack of a valve all together.

As a result, stomach acid constantly came up into his esophagus, paralyzing it, and making it nearly impossible to swallow food. Matt lost a lot of weight, had heartburn that was at first consistent and eventually unrelenting, and fell behind in school until he eventually had to drop out.

Days, weeks, and months became defined by doctor's appointments. Matt and his mom began to joke that the only quality time they spent together was in waiting rooms and hospital beds. Amidst the frustration and exhaustion, however, Matt was drawn to the diligence of his doctors, namely his endocrinologist, Dr. Minh Mach, MD.

Dr. Mach's kindness, compassion and persistence to ensure Matt received the best care sparked a desire in Matt to pay it forward, to find a way to help people the way he had been helped.

Endocrinologists primarily deal with metabolism—how the body turns food into energy—and often have degrees in fields like biology, chemistry, and medicine. Having some time away from school, Matt began to research similar professions in the medical field, wondering if there was a good fit for him.

As a start, while Matt began seeing a GI doctor recommended by Dr. Mach, he enrolled at the College of the Canyons in Santa Clarita, California, to pursue an associate of science in both biology and mathematics. But the marriage of the two processes was not easy. The doctor ran even more tests, some unpleasant and invasive, leaving Matt exhausted. This made focusing on school difficult and Matt struggled to keep his grades up. But he was determined to see a life on the other side of the illness, and determined to put footwork into his future as soon as possible, so he fought through it. Then, when the doctor determined there was no other course of action except surgery, they scheduled the procedure during a break in classes.

Afterward, the doctors told him that while the surgery was complicated, it was successful, thus giving Matt the green light to finally move forward with his goals.

Matt finished his degrees at College of the Canyons, then applied and was accepted to the University of California, Davis to study pharmaceutical chemistry.

University of Florida Health defines pharmaceutical chemistry as "the study of drugs [including] drug discovery, delivery, [and] absorption," and notes that "studying pharmaceutical chemistry allows students to contribute to life-saving remedies, enhance the speed of delivery of new medications, and help others."[3]

It seemed like the perfect fit for Matt. It gave him the opportunity to do the life-changing work Dr. Mach had inspired in him, while leaning on his strengths to work diligently behind the scenes.

When looking for schools that offered this degree, Matt came across a number of programs offering a bachelor of science in biochemistry with a *specialization* in pharmaceuticals. But University of California, Davis was one of the only programs he found that had a specific *degree* in pharmaceutical chemistry. And so, the choice was made.

[MATT]

Ellen

In China, children are required by law to receive nine years of education. This includes six years of primary school, which usually starts at age six, and three years of junior secondary school. Once children complete junior secondary school (or junior middle school), they are given two options:[4]

1. Senior middle school, which is similar to high school in the United States. Students often take this route if they are hoping to go to college and pursue a degree.
2. Vocational middle school, which is similar to trade school. Students taking this route receive two to four years of training in a specialized area of study or skill.

Throughout primary and secondary school, Ellen had a lot of friends. She was talkative and outgoing and loved meeting new people. She also loved learning English, which is why she chose to attend a vocational middle school that specialized in the language.

In China, many signs, menus, and billboards are printed in English, so she liked the familiarity her education gave her to the language and looked forward to a deeper understanding that could hopefully benefit her in the future.

After she finished secondary school, however, her English studies waned.

She moved to Shanghai with her aunt and uncle from next door and got a job as a telemarketer selling stock certificates. She made cold calls and got hung up on, encountering people in their worst moments and foulest moods. It was exhausting, unforgiving work, leaving her little energy or motivation to study in her spare time. Coworkers came

[ELLEN]

and went, unable to handle the pressures and negativities of the job, but she tried to be patient and remain grateful for the job itself and the support it gave her financially.

Outside of work, Ellen's life was good. She still attended church regularly with Chris and her aunt and uncle, and she was taking classes at her church in the hopes of getting baptized. The way Ellen describes it, to become a Christian in China—or at least the way she experienced it—you are required to meet with the pastor of your church in order learn the basics of the Bible, and the core beliefs of Christianity before you are able to be baptized. Unfortunately, these classes were only offered on Saturdays. This posed no problem initially, as her job at the telemarketing agency gave her weekends off. But when she eventually left that position and started working for Lee, a popular retail chain, she worked every single Saturday.

At Lee, Ellen was much happier in her work life. As a sales associate, she was able to interact with customers one on one, fitting them in jeans and helping them find whatever they needed. The position allowed her social skills to shine and the customers loved her. Oftentimes they would ask for her contact information as they left, so they could call to plan their shopping trips around her work schedule. One customer even asked Ellen to be in her wedding.

While the work was fulfilling, her schedule was rigid. Weeks and months would go by with Ellen unable to have a shift covered or switched, making it almost impossible to attend the baptism classes. Even so, Ellen remained calm, because although the completion of the classes meant something in the way of pronouncing her faith publicly, she had already done so privately. She had accepted Jesus as her savior and believed in His plans for her.

Coming from a home that was not loving or accepting of either Ellen the person or, especially, Ellen the *girl*, she had found a home in the church and in Jesus.

"Every time I went to church," Ellen says, "My heart felt peaceful. It was no longer empty. It was full. I felt joy. For the first time, I no longer felt alone."

Ellen gained a firm foundation of faith. She'd seen God deliver her into the arms of her aunt and uncle, into this new life in Shanghai, and she trusted that if it was in His plans for her to get baptized, He would intervene at the perfect time to help her finish the classes.

In the meantime, she continued going to church with her aunt and uncle every Sunday and always left feeling refreshed and inspired. She also maintained a busy work schedule that continued to challenge her and introduce her to customers that turned into friends.

After a while, a new girl started working at the store. Her shifts alternated so she occasionally worked with Ellen, and in time they got to know each other. One day, as they were talking, Ellen told her about her struggles to find a Saturday off to finish her baptism classes, and without a second thought, the girl offered to switch her shifts for as long as necessary.

Ellen finished her classes soon after.

Matt

For years leading up to college, Matt had always wanted to study abroad. Being anxious and shy by nature, the idea was far out of his comfort zone, but having gone on a number of mission trips growing up, he was drawn to learning about other cultures and seeing the world, so he was determined to push himself.

While studying at Cal Lutheran, there were only two study abroad programs available for his degree: one in Jordan and one in South Korea. For months he agonized over which one to choose, never feeling particularly drawn to or confident in either choice.

When he left Cal Lutheran and arrived at UC Davis, he immediately began to research their study abroad program. As it turned out, they only had one option: Taipei, Taiwan. He signed up immediately.

In preparation for his quarter abroad, Matt purchased books and online lessons to help him learn Chinese. He also downloaded the language learning app Hello Talk, in the hopes of meeting people in Taiwan before leaving home.

Hello Talk is the combination of an educational app, like Duolingo, a social media app, like Instagram or Facebook, and a text messaging app like WhatsApp. After downloading the app, you select which country you are from, your native language, and which language you are hoping to learn. Once your profile is created, you have access to a number of tools:

1. A "learn" section, where you can practice new words, listen to stories in the language you're learning, and sign up for online classes to help with pronunciation.
2. A "search" section where you can find people to chat and learn with.
3. A "moments" section which allows you to share photos and posts, as well as interact with those shared by others.
4. And a "talk" section that allows you to keep track of conversations, send voice memos, make voice and video calls, and send doodles.

As a whole, Hello Talk can act as a kind of community for those looking to connect with people all around the world.

In the three months leading up to his trip, Matt made five friends through Hello Talk, all of whom lived in Taiwan and graciously helped him with his introductory Chinese. Once he arrived in Taiwan, these friends gave Matt connections in the city, providing him with personal tour guides to the best cafés, concerts, and other local hot spots—not to mention a reputable tattoo parlor where Matt went on his birthday to get his first tattoo: a ship on his bicep.

"I fell in love with the city," Matt says. "The people, the food, it was all wonderful."

But then, just as soon as the program started, it was over. Three months flew by and before he knew it Matt was back home. With one year left at UC Davis, he put his head down and worked hard, grateful for his time in Taiwan and ready for whatever came next.

Ellen

Being a few years removed from school, Ellen wanted to get back into studying English.

While her job kept her busy, with multiple ten-hour workdays per week, she had aspirations of traveling the world and knew that speaking English could be a huge advantage.

Oftentimes as she made her way into work, she would see people passing out fliers on the street, advertising English classes. (Picture the people you might see selling products at kiosks in your local shopping mall, or those collecting signatures, asking for donations, or selling cookies outside of grocery stores, at busy intersections, etc.) Ellen did not want to be rude, but she also didn't have time to stop each and every day, so she usually politely declined their offer and kept moving. One day however, she took a flier for a company called "Wall Street English" and stuck it in her purse. It sat there for a few days, shuffling around with her wallet and keys, first forgotten, then ignored—if only to put up the slightest protest against the workers who waved the fliers in her face day in and day out. But when she finally pulled it out to take a good look at it, she got curious.

"TEST YOUR ENGLISH" it said in bold letters.

How much did she remember from school? She wondered.

What kind of starting point was she looking at?

A website was given at the bottom of the flier and she logged on to take the test. At the end, before she was given her results, it asked for her phone number and email, which she reluctantly provided.

The next day, she received a call from the company, giving her the full pitch for continuing her education and inviting her to come visit the learning center. On her next day off, Ellen made an appointment with one of the instructors, who ultimately convinced her to start taking classes.

Soon after, the instructor encouraged Ellen to work on her pronunciation, as this seemed to be her biggest challenge. Her recommendation? A language learning app called Hello Talk.

Matt

Two weeks after graduating from UC Davis with his degree in pharmaceutical chemistry, Matt got a job as a specimen associate at a clinical trial laboratory, where he stored samples of drugs and sent them to the labs to be tested. The job was hard and not quite what he thought it was going to be. There was something about it that didn't quite feel like the right fit.

Some days, Matt thought of his time in the hospital and how the kindness of the nurses and doctors had inspired him to find a job that allowed him to help people. *Maybe I should have chosen nursing*, he wondered. *Or maybe I should go back to school for it now*. Other days he wondered whether he should have stuck to computer science, as that had always felt like a good option and had been a continued passion throughout his life.

In the meantime, he continued to work hard and was eventually promoted to a lead position, which opened the door to a long-term career path within the field. While the steadiness was encouraging, it also made his curiosity about leaving, and the window of time to do so, seem more pressing.

Outside of work, Matt remained active on Hello Talk and often checked in with his friends from Taiwan. But he often wondered if his continued pursuit of learning Chinese was pointless. He did not foresee a return to Taiwan or anticipate a trip to any other Chinese speaking countries, so he considered taking up a new language instead. Many of his coworkers were Filipino and spoke Tagalog, so he felt encouraged to go that route. But each time he opened the page to change his language preference, he felt a strong call from the Lord: "Keep learning Chinese. I have a reason."

Why? Matt wondered.

He found Chinese difficult and frustrating. Leading up to his quarter abroad, he'd had special motivation and drive to learn as much as he could and connect with as many people as possible. But now, working a job he was unsure about, feeling unsteady about his future, and confused of what his next move should be, he wanted to start something new, to try something else. But each time he prayed about it, he got the same answer.

Keep learning Chinese.

Just. Keep. Learning.

So he did.

And one day, as he scrolled through his feed on Hello Talk, looking at photos, chatting with other friendly faces, and trying his best to *just keep learning*, something caught his eye. A post that, as he began to translate it, he quickly realized was a Bible verse.

> "Finally, be strong in the Lord and in his mighty power. Put on the full armor of God, so that you can take your stand against the devil's schemes."
>
> — *Ephesians 6:10–11*

He commented on the post, excited to meet a native Chinese speaker who was also a Christian. She replied back, matching his enthusiasm to meet an English-speaking Christian.

"It's nice to meet you!" he said. "I'm Matt."

"It's nice to meet you too!" she replied. "I'm Ellen."

Ellen

Not long after Ellen completed her baptism classes, she returned to her hometown to see her family. Her father, whom she'd had contact with over the years, had died of lung cancer, and she'd come for the Qingming festival or "Tomb Sweeping Day." In traditional Chinese culture, this is a holiday in which family members would methodically clean up the tomb or gravesite of a loved one, but with burial not only being uncommon, but illegal in many parts of China, more modern celebrations of this day aim solely to pay respect to lost loved ones.

While in town, Ellen also had hopes of sharing the gospel with her family. Growing up, her parents and siblings had often discouraged her from visiting the neighbors (whom she would eventually call her aunt and uncle) because they were Christians. They warned Ellen that Christians were bad, crazy people and that she'd do better to stay away from them.

But Ellen felt drawn to her neighbors. Before she ever attended church with them, she recognized an unfamiliar goodness in their family. Then, when she did start attending their church, she took additional notice of the unwarranted kindness they showed her, and the way they cared for her like she was part of their family. It made her curious about the kind of impact Jesus could have on her own life.

"When I started going to church," she says, "I could see that goodness in everyone. Everyone was so nice and caring. They made me feel so welcome. Every time I would go to church, my heart would stop feeling empty. Sometimes I would just start crying and didn't know why. I just felt so peaceful in church and so I knew that it wasn't a bad place like my family had said."

Having finished her baptism classes (though not yet baptized due to scheduling conflicts), Ellen returned home carrying a Bible and wearing a cross necklace, hopeful to share this newfound faith and peace with her family. But upon entering her house, her mom told her to take off the necklace and throw her Bible in the trash. Her family rejected all attempts to share her faith, saying she had joined a cult and would be cast out of their family.

Heartbroken, Ellen prayed for her family. She asked God to speak to them, to touch their hearts and open their eyes to the love he had shown her. Then she returned to Shanghai.

* * *

As a tradition, every Sunday after church, Ellen, her aunt and uncle, and their kids, went out to eat at a Mexican restaurant nearby. One afternoon, as they sat eating and talking, she received a message on Hello Talk from a boy who had liked the Bible verse she had posted earlier in the day. She was excited to meet an American who could not only help her with her English, but was a Christian as well. She responded to his message and then posted a picture of the restaurant where they were eating.

"You like Mexican food?!" the boy replied. "And you have it in China?!"

Ellen laughed, curious. The boy went on to tell her about the childhood dreams he had of becoming a chef and opening a Mexican restaurant of his own. This excited Ellen, as food had always been a passion of hers as well. They began to talk about other dreams they had, like where they wanted to travel, music they enjoyed, foods they wanted to try, and Bible verses that spoke to them.

At first, they just sent text messages. But soon they sent photos and voice recordings, and eventually started video chatting whenever they could.

They both kept Pleco, a Chinese-to-English dictionary app, close at hand, using it to help fill in the gaps of translation. Even though Matt was in Southern California, Ellen was in Shanghai, and the fifteen-hour time difference made their schedules run at almost completely opposite intervals, they made talking to each other a priority. They memorized each other's schedules, waking up early to say goodnight and staying awake just long enough to say good morning.

"I was exhausted every single day," Matt says. "One time I was so tired I dropped my phone on my face."

They carried on like that for months, unsure of where they were going, but each day they grew more confident that wherever it was, they wanted to go there together.

Matt

Growing up, Matt had a shining example of a loving, healthy marriage. His parents, John and Karen, met in middle school and got married in 1979.

"My parents showed me how to live a good and godly life," Matt says. "You could always see the love they had for each other and the love they had for Jesus."

As a result, Matt found himself to be very picky when it came to dating. He admired his parents and strived to have a marriage like theirs, so he set a standard that relationships would need to live up to and didn't want to settle for less.

In high school, Matt began a relationship with a girl whom he was very excited about. Over time, however, she became verbally and psychologically abusive. But even when he realized how unhealthy the relationship was, he had trouble ending it for good. His self-esteem plummeted to an all-time low and his hopes for a fresh start dwindled. He was discouraged and hurt, worried he might never find that perfect person for him, and he fell into a dark place. But his family got behind him, not only to pray for him but to encourage him to lean on God to find his way forward.

"I remember one day," Matt says, "sitting in prayer with God and talking about the whole situation. I wanted to know His plans for me and what I should do. I remember hearing him say, almost like a parent to a child on Christmas morning, 'I have someone very special for you.' I could feel the excitement. It was like he could hardly contain himself. 'I have someone perfect for you,' He said, 'and at the right time, you'll know it. Just be patient.'"

After that, Matt's propensity for pickiness sharpened. As he waited for that feeling, that assuredness, he put his head down and focused on school.

At the same time, Matt's mom Karen prayed for his future spouse, the same way she'd done for all of her kids since they were young. She prayed diligently and patiently, asking God to ensure Matt's future spouse was safe and cared for. She asked God to put his hand on her life and weave her path towards Matt, so that they might find each other and create a new life together.

Matt felt confident in her prayer and his own. He felt encouraged and allowed the fear of the future to fall away. He knew his perfect person was out there and he was willing to be patient to find her.

Ellen

It was Ellen's grandfather who introduced Ellen's father to her mother. As part of his job in the family planning division, he visited many villages surrounding his own. On one such trip he heard about a woman who was well liked in the community. She was respected and unmarried, and as such he thought she would be a good match for his son. So, he encouraged his son to pursue her.

In time, when a proposal seemed appropriate, Ellen's grandfather and grandmother sent Ellen's mother betrothal gifts. Typical of a traditional Chinese proposal, they sent things like alcohol, cookies, cigarettes, and tea as a sign of respect for her family and an encouragement for the match.

Soon after, they were married.

Thinking back on her parents' marriage, Ellen describes their relationship as "so-so."

"I think they loved each other," she says, "but they fought often so it was hard to tell."

Ellen also points out that it is less common for couples in China to marry for love, or to remain in love the way she has seen relationships portrayed in Western society.

"Often in China," she says, "relationships are more functional than romantic."

Dating is also far less common. When I asked if she'd had any romantic relationships in high school, Ellen shook her head. For her, school was marked as far more important than dating. Her parents were adamant that she do well on her exams and finish school rather than wasting time on dating.

Even so, Ellen constantly prayed to find the "right" person.

As she made her way through school, moved to Shanghai, got her job at Lee, and finished her Bible classes, Ellen constantly prayed for God to send her a good man. And she felt encouraged when God told her to keep being patient.

"He would say, 'I have someone special for you,'" she recalls, "'One day you are going to meet the perfect person. Just be patient.'"

* * *

One night, as she stayed awake talking to Matt, Ellen nervously told him about her longstanding prayer and the consistent answer she'd received over the years.

I have someone special for you.

"Woah," Matt replied, almost 6,500 miles away. "That's the exact same thing He said to me." Goosebumps crept up their arms and an assuredness settled in both of their hearts.

But there was still one major step they had to take: they had to meet in person.

FINDING GOD
IN THE DETAILS

Now we have the road map of how Matt and Ellen's separate paths came to run parallel.

Eyes without a foundation of faith might call on coincidence, luck, or fate. But eyes trained or focused on God's plans will notice His hand on their lives and the perfect timing in which all of the puzzle pieces fell into place.

Let's zoom out and consider the what-ifs.

Oftentimes, we use what-ifs to encourage dreams and goals for our future, or to look negatively and regretfully at our past. But here they can showcase God's ability to give purpose to each and every moment of our lives.

What if Matt didn't grow up in a Christian family? What if he didn't learn to lean on God and to trust in His plans from a young age?

What if Matt's family friend never offered to buy him a computer? Or Matt said no when the offer came parlayed with the requirement to build it himself?

What if Matt never got sick? Never dropped out of Cal Lutheran University and in turn finished his degree in computer science?

What if Matt had been assigned a different endocrinologist? One that didn't inspire him to help others or to pursue a degree in the medical field?

What if he had studied abroad in Jordan or South Korea? Or what if he never went abroad at all?

What if he decided a degree in biochemistry with a specialization in pharmaceuticals was close enough to his desired field, and he applied to a host of other universities?

What if UC Davis had more than one study abroad program? And what if he didn't choose to study in Taiwan so he never had to learn Chinese?

Some of these what-ifs may well have been asked by Matt or his friends and family as he went through challenging seasons. But looking back now, we can see that any change to any of these details would have put Matt on a completely different path. It would have given him a different life, and a different future.

Sometimes, when we go through struggles, darkness, or impossible loss, we ask God why. Why am I going through this? Why did you let this happen? Why can't I go *that* way, or do *this*, or be *different*? While God does not find joy in our pain or suffering, He does give purpose to those parts of our lives. He gives purpose to our darkest moments, biggest mistakes, and greatest regrets. And He *does* give answers to those hard questions, but not always right away.

Romans 8:28 NLT says, "And we know that God causes everything to work together for the good of those who love God and are called according to his purpose for them."

He causes *everything* to work together. Not just the good parts. Not just the happy or the "easy" parts. He doesn't work exclusively in the moments when we feel confident, safe, loved, and full of unfailing faith. He causes everything to work together for good. Even things that break our hearts. Even things we wish would have turned out differently. Even things that bring us to our knees asking "why?" Or "why not?" Or "what if?"

When we remember that truth, we can start to see that God has already planned for the what-ifs. He has already put us on the path that will quiet the what-ifs that define our past and create the what-ifs that inspire our future.

* * *

"What if I started studying kung fu?" a man once asked himself.

"What if I study Chinese medicine?"

"What if I marry the woman I love?"

"What if we buy a house in this small town in China?"

"What if we have children and raise them to be kind human beings who honor God?"

And what if, in time, that man became a kung fu master and a Chinese medicine doctor, giving him good standing in the community. What if he married a kind woman and they had four children? What if they bought a house in Guangdong, next to a family with five children? What if they invited the youngest daughter of that family over to celebrate her birthday because it landed one day after their son's? What if they brought her to church with them and taught her about Jesus?

What if? God stirred in that man's heart long before Ellen was born.

"What if?" asked Ellen as she considered moving to Shanghai; as she applied to Lee's retail store; and as she called the number on the flier advertising English language classes.

"What if?" asked the creators at Apple as they went about creating the smart phone that would first be released in 2007.

"What if?" they asked again as they created the app store that would be released a year later.

"What if?" Hello Talk creator Zackery Ngai asked as he launched his new language learning app in 2012.

"What if?" Ellen thought as she downloaded the app five years later to help with her pronunciation.

"What if?" Matt thought as he messaged the girl who posted a Bible verse in Chinese.

"What if?" Ellen thought as she messaged him back.

* * *

God works all things together for good. There are so many pieces we don't see, don't understand, or don't recognize His presence in. But He ties everything—and everyone—together. He is always near. He is always on the move. And He is always listening to the prayers of our hearts.

"What if?" you may have asked when you picked up this book. God has a plan for that as well.

PIECES COME TOGETHER

Matt & Ellen: Long-Distance

After their initial interaction on Hello Talk, Matt and Ellen started communicating regularly. First a few times a week, then every couple days, and then every day. Living in different time zones, on opposite ends of the world, this wasn't easy.

Shanghai is 15 hours ahead of Los Angeles. When Matt was getting ready for bed in Los Angeles at 11:00 pm on a Thursday, it was 2:00 pm on Friday for Ellen and she was at work. And when Ellen was getting ready for bed at 10:00 pm that Friday, Matt was waking up for work at 7:00 a.m.

Still, they found a way. They even found humor in it.

"One time," Ellen says, "as I was going to bed, I texted him 'good morning.' When he didn't answer back right away, I texted him again. Turns out, he had slept through his alarm but my messages woke him up!"

As text messages gave way to voice messages and voice messages paved the way for video chatting, Matt and Ellen began to realize their connection was special. They wanted to meet in person, to test the relationship outside the digital space, to see if it had more than just casual potential.

So, in March of 2018, about eight months after they met, Matt booked a flight to Shanghai.

* * *

Leading up to Matt's visit, Ellen studied English day and night, hoping to make up for lost time. She invented conversations they might have and practiced answering questions he might ask. Matt did the same with Chinese. They sat on opposite ends of the world, counting down the days until they would see each other, diligently studying the many words they might use to express that excitement.

At first, Matt's family was hesitant about his leaving. They were nervous to watch their son fly halfway around the world to meet someone for the first time. But they saw how much he liked her. They could hear it in the way he talked about her and recognized the connection Matt and Ellen shared in their faith, and so they gave him their blessing. They trusted Matt and they trusted God. The same was true for Ellen's aunt and uncle. They trusted her. The fact that Matt was a Christian brought them peace and they believed he could make Ellen happy.

What if? Both families must have wondered.

Matt & Ellen: In the Same Time Zone

As Matt stood in the immigration line after his plane landed in Shanghai, he was nervous. His near 18-hour flight had left him jet-lagged and exhausted, and the slow-moving line seemed almost too much to bear. But as he stepped forward, each time closer to the window, he also buzzed with excitement.

Every message, every call, every video chat had led to this moment. The moment he would finally get to see Ellen in person, to exist with her in the same time zone, experiencing days as they started and finished, together.

What will she be like?

What if I don't recognize her?

Meanwhile, as Ellen stood on the other side of the gate, she too was nervous.

Having never traveled internationally, she had no idea how long it took for someone to move through the airport immigration process and wondered what was taking so long. With each passing minute, it felt like her heart beat faster and her mind raced with questions.

What is he going to say?

What will I say?

When Matt made it through immigration, he popped into the nearest bathroom. He washed his face and sprayed on some cologne. He looked at himself in the mirror, knowing everything was about to change.

Ellen's heart jumped as she saw Matt walking towards the gate.

Matt's heart flooded with relief as he instantly recognized Ellen.

Wow, she is so beautiful, Matt thought.

He is so handsome.

Ellen smiled.

"I swear her face seemed to glow," Matt says. "Just by looking at her, I could see Jesus in her."

"Watching him walk towards me," Ellen echoes, "I could sense that he was a man of God. I thought, I'm going to marry that man."

This is the one, they both thought. The one God told them to wait for. The answer to every prayer they'd prayed. The answer to the prayers Matt's mom, and Ellen's aunt and uncle had prayed.

As they walked towards each other, their hearts pounded.

"Hello," Matt said.

"Hi," Ellen replied.

Timidness bounced between them, leaving them both speechless. But with a hug, their nerves faded and excitement took charge. Ellen asked about Matt's flight and they laughed as they shared the mutual toll that waiting had taken on them. They took a taxi to the hotel Matt was staying in for the week so he could drop off his bags, and then set out into the city.

As they walked around Shanghai, the conversation came easy. Matt and Ellen fell into the rhythm they'd found while texting and video chatting, and were grateful to have Pleco, the Chinese-to-English dictionary app, on hand to ensure nothing got lost in translation.

For the next week, Matt and Ellen got to spend a lot of time together. Ellen introduced Matt to the food she grew up on and they explored the city, visiting tourist favorites like the Shanghai Aquarium, Yu Garden, and Shanghai Disneyland Park. However, Ellen's work schedule was still strict and demanding, so when she was unavailable Matt spent time with Chris (the son of Ellen's aunt and uncle). Reminiscent of his time in Taiwan, Matt loved being given a tour of the city by a local, but more than that, he loved being given a window into Ellen's world.

As they walked around, Matt and Chris had time to talk, giving them both adequate time to gain their footing

[MATT AND ELLEN IN SHANGHAI]

in what could become a very serious relationship. Matt was given a glimpse into Ellen's family, hearing about her life from someone who grew up beside her and witnessed her obstacles and triumphs firsthand. And Chris got the opportunity to meet Matt and learn about the man who had flown all the way from California to meet Ellen.

In a way, they were vetting each other, as they understood the importance of the other, both in Ellen's life and their respective lives going forward. They bonded over their faith and they were excited at what the future might hold.

On the Sunday Matt was set to fly back to California, Ellen took him to her church and then to the Mexican restaurant she'd posted a picture of on Hello Talk. The same restaurant that made Matt double take after he saw her initial post of the Bible verse. It was surreal to be in a place that sparked the start of their relationship, to no longer be two strangers chatting online but two people who had fallen in love and believed that God had designed them for one another.

When the time came for Matt to return home, the peace in having found each other and the confidence in the bright future they had together competed hard with the anguish of being separated again. The distance threatened uncertainty and doubt, but Matt and Ellen clung to each other, and to their faith, praying that they would see each other again soon. And then, just as they'd shared the anticipation of meeting, they felt the joint heartbreak of saying goodbye. Matt sat on the plane, drained and nauseous, and Ellen sat on a bench outside the airport unable to hold back her tears.

[SHANGHAI: VIEW OF PUDONG FROM THE BUND]

When Matt landed back in California, he texted Ellen to let her know he was safe. Ellen had just woken up and was getting ready for work, while Matt was fighting to stay awake until after the sun went down. They were back on a schedule they knew well, but they didn't want it to stay that way for long.

Matt & Ellen: Next Steps

After Matt's visit to Shanghai, Matt and Ellen began to talk about marriage. It was a cautious conversation at first, as they hadn't known each other for long. But the more they talked about it, the more confident they became.

They both felt drawn to each other in a way that went beyond physical and even emotional attraction. They felt a call to pursue this relationship, and to the faith that it strengthened in both of them.

Before they moved forward, however, they made one promise above all else.

"We will always put God first."

They knew that in entering into any kind of relationship, especially a marriage, it was vital for them to agree on what was most important. Agreeing to put God first in everything gave them a foundation to fall back on, and a guiding light in times of trial.

Unbeknownst to them, this promise would prove to be a life raft over the following few years, both in the anticipated tides of inexperience that come with any new marriage, and in the raging waters that they never saw coming.

* * *

Within a few months, marriage was not only in their plans but budding on the horizon. As such, being a US citizen, Matt had to start taking the necessary steps that would allow him to marry Ellen and move to China. But the process proved rather complicated.

First, he had to fill out a Single Status Affidavit. This document states you are single and thus not currently married, allowing you to get married. Once completed, Matt took the document to be notarized, then verified and authenticated by the court of Los Angeles. This cleared it on the American side of things, allowing him to forward it to the Chinese consulate, where it would be translated, verified, and authenticated a second time.

Next he had to get a visa.

In China, there are five main types of visas.[5] A tourist visa (also known as an L visa), a non-commercial visit visa (F visa), a business visa (M visa), a work visa (Z visa), and a student visa (X visa). Matt would need a Z visa.

But first, he needed a job. Once he had proof of a job, also known as a Notification of Work Permit,[6] he could submit his application along with his passport and other supporting documents for the Z visa. So he started looking for jobs in Shanghai.

As he scrolled through job postings, Matt heard a persistent call to teach, which was both surprising and strange to him. Having always been soft spoken and shy, Matt had never imagined himself in a teaching position, let alone in a foreign country. But English teachers are constantly in demand in China, and as he continued to look for job opportunities, these not only seemed to be the ones most readily available, but those that stood out and called for his attention. It was as if God was underlining and circling them, drawing arrows and running a highlighter across the page. Eventually, the call became too loud to ignore.

So, Matt enrolled in a program to earn his TEFL (Teaching English as a Foreign Language) certificate. The 100-hour requirement took him about a month to complete, but once finished he created and formatted a new resume, applied for a few jobs, and received a request for an interview within a few days.

It seemed as if things were moving both slowly and quickly at the same time. As a result, Matt remained steadfast in prayer, constantly asking God for guidance. While he could see some of the blessings God was putting in his path, he was also very aware at how far he was moving outside of his comfort zone. He would be leaving his family, his friends, and all sense of familiarity. He would also potentially be starting a teaching job that put him at the forefront of attention, something completely different than cooking, computer science, and pharmaceutical chemistry, which had all placed him safely behind the scenes. As a result, Matt was constantly put at the crossroads of trusting God and doubting Him.

Proverbs 3:5–6 says, "Trust in the LORD with all your heart and lean not on your own understanding; in all your ways submit to him, and he will make your paths straight."

The Message translation puts it this way: "Trust GOD from the bottom of your heart; don't try to figure out everything on your own. Listen for GOD's voice in everything you do, everywhere you go; he's the one who will keep you on track."

So Matt trusted God. And he listened. Through each step of the application process, he remained in prayer, asking God if this is the step He would have him take. He wanted God to truly be, as Psalm 119:105 says, the "light unto his path" because by all accounts, this path was entirely unexpected, unpredictable, and, seemingly, far unfinished.

With this in mind, almost immediately after an initial interview with a teaching job in Shanghai, Matt knew that school wasn't where he belonged. While the interview had gone well and Matt was offered the job, he felt a hesitancy to accept—not based on fear, but in faith. On the surface, the job seemed great. It would allow him to work with young children and was located close to where Ellen lived. They could stay in her apartment and start their married life together in close proximity to Ellen's aunt and uncle. But as Matt prayed about it, he knew it wasn't the right fit, so he eventually turned it down and kept looking.

Meanwhile, Ellen was still studying English at Wall Street English, so she offered to ask around to see if there were any teaching jobs available within the company. Using the connections of a few colleagues and friends, she forwarded Matt's resume to the manager at the Shanghai branch, and within a few days he received a request for an interview. When he accepted, they scheduled an interview for two weeks later.

With this on the calendar, both Matt and Ellen felt optimistic. Things were coming together. Their plans were coming to fruition. God's faithfulness was opening doors left and right.

But He was not finished yet.

As the date of the interview drew closer, Matt again felt a call. A curiosity. A push. He went back on the Wall Street English company website, not knowing what he was looking for, but sure there was something to find. And then, there it was, highlighted and underlined.

Matt clicked on the job posting.

It was a teaching position, more or less identical to the one he had an interview scheduled for. But this job was located at the Guangzhou branch, which was almost 900 miles from Shanghai.

Matt had never been to Guangzhou. He didn't have any connection to it other than the fact that it was only about 50 miles from Ellen's hometown—a place that had shown her such unkindness and neglect. The last time she'd been there, her family had cast her out for becoming a Christian.

Could this really be what God had planned for them?

Could this really be the right place, the right job, the right path for them to take?

Unbeknownst to Matt at the time, Ellen had good memories in Guangzhou. It had provided an escape from her hometown when she was younger. And even though she wanted to stay in Shanghai, she recognized the uneasiness in Matt as he'd considered previous job postings, as well as the undeniable *call* that came with this one. She prioritized staying together over everything, and was excited at every job prospect Matt pursued, as it meant they were closer to starting their lives together.

"I would have gone anywhere," Ellen says. "And I thought that if God was calling us to Guangzhou it must be for a reason.

So, Matt applied. Within a matter of hours, he got a request for a same day interview, and by the end, Matt was offered the job and accepted it with confidence.

Soon after, Matt's visa application was approved.

By this time, it was the end of August and the position started in October. Suddenly, everything moved in fast forward.

Matt & Ellen: The Marriage Book

In September, Matt booked another flight to Shanghai, this time a one-way ticket. Matt and Ellen had openly discussed marriage and wanted to be married before they moved in together, so they planned get married shortly after Matt arrived. Still, Matt wanted to surprise Ellen with a formal proposal. So over the course of the next month, as Matt packed up his life in Los Angeles, he also mapped out the perfect proposal in China.

In doing research on Guangzhou, Matt found a park with a scenic lake and paddleboats for rent. Ellen had never been on a paddleboat, so Matt thought that after a ride around the lake, he could reach down into his bag, pretending to grab his phone, and pull out the box with the ring. Or rather, the Ring Pop.

Matt had found a ring box that was multilayered, allowing him to add a playful element to the proposal. When he opened the box, a Ring Pop—as in, the delicious, sugary, candy accessory—would be sitting on top. A small LED light installed in the box would cast a spotlight onto the ring, making it sparkle and glisten. He hoped it would make Ellen laugh before he showed her the real ring, which was safely tucked on the lower level of the box.

With the plan in place, his stuff packed, and all of his paperwork cleared, Matt flew to Shanghai. Ellen met him at the airport, and then the two of them flew to Guangzhou together.

Matt arrived at the end of September, two days before National Day and the start of Golden Week, which is a seven-day public holiday that celebrates China's independence and emergence as a nation state.[7] This meant that, alongside many businesses and schools, the government office of the department of marriage would be closed both on National Day and the entirety of the following week.

Similar to obtaining a marriage license and exchanging vows in a courthouse, the department of marriage in China is where a couple can register their marriage, making it legal and official. Many couples opt to hold a ceremony with friends and family at a later date, and Matt and Ellen had this idea in mind. But they wanted their marriage to be official before then, and they wanted to be married before they moved in together. So, with everything set to close for the next seven days, and Matt's job starting in two weeks, Matt knew that he would have to arrive, propose, and then get married on the very next day.

Needless to say, the schedule was very tight. When they arrived at the park, the paddleboats were closed. So they started walking, with Ellen looking at the scenery and Matt wearing a backpack with the ring box inside, trying to salvage his plan as the already palpable time crunch got crunchier. He took Ellen's hand, hopeful he could find another perfect spot, and then happened upon a dock that walked out over the water and under a gazebo. Beautiful green trees and lush flowers surrounded them with color, giving them a serene place to sit down and talk. After a while, Matt felt like he'd reached the moment. He pulled out the box, opened the top to reveal the Ring Pop and Ellen gasped.

"Is this candy?!" she said, excited. "Can I eat it?"

Matt laughed, nodding, and she delighted in this before realizing that he was proposing.

"Oh!" she said, as he revealed the real ring beneath the candy. "Yes! Yes, I will marry you!"

—

[THE PROPOSAL SITE]

[GUANGZHOU CITY AT NIGHT]

The next day, they hopped on a train to Ellen's hometown in Guangdong, as it is required by law in China for a Chinese citizen to be married in the location their hukou (or household register) is registered. Previously, Ellen could have applied for a Shanghai hukou, if she had met the necessary requirements to do so (which include a steady job, a minimum period of social security payments, and a minimum continuous residency).[8] However, at the time, her hukou was still registered in the city she was born. It was a two-hour train ride, and both Matt and Ellen remember it with humor, as jet lag had started to take its full effect on Matt, making him feel as though the two-hour train ride was upwards of seven.

Once in her hometown, they headed straight to the marriage registration office, where they'd called and made an appointment after the proposal. By the time they arrived, it was early afternoon, and the offices were set to close within a matter of hours. Matt and Ellen presented their required documents, including Matt's Single Status Affidavit, Ellen's equivalent certificate of marriageability, Ellen's hukou, and Matt's passport. Almost immediately, the government official pulled aside Matt's passport and handed it back, saying that before they could proceed, it would need to be translated into Chinese.

Matt and Ellen gathered all of their things and rushed over to the local notary public. When they approached the woman at the front desk, she was cold and passive, explaining unenthusiastically that the translation would take a week to complete. Matt and Ellen exchanged glances, worried, and then Ellen turned back to the woman and explained their situation. She laid everything out on the line, not knowing if it would pay off, or if her honesty would somehow backfire. Ellen stood vulnerable in front of the woman, trying to convey to her how important this day was, trying to be hopeful, but not expecting much in return. Remarkably however, as Ellen told her story, the woman's face changed. Her heart softened and her eyes lit up.

"I can have it done in one hour," she said. And then she took the passport and set to work on it straight away.

Shocked by her graciousness, Matt and Ellen left the notary public and went out to lunch, amazed at the moment of calm God was able to give them on such a stressful day. They sat, enjoying each other's company in the warm September weather, for the first time feeling the excitement of their impending marriage rather than the stress of the process. And when they returned to the notary, the woman handed them Matt's passport, with a smile, and wished them well.

Back at the marriage registration office, Matt and Ellen presented their documents and filled out the remaining paperwork, then they had their pictures taken and prepared to state their vows. The vows were traditional and written in Chinese, so while Ellen read them aloud, Matt was not required to. Instead, the vows were read on his behalf and at the conclusion Matt was asked to simply agree, which he did. To conclude the ceremony, they had their fingerprints taken and were then asked to take a seat as their marriage books were created.

Like a marriage license that is typical of Western culture, a marriage book, which is similar in size and shape to a passport, is issued to both the bride and groom after a Chinese wedding ceremony. The book marks the beginning of the couple's marriage and features pictures of the couple on their wedding day.

[MARRIAGE BOOKS]

As Matt and Ellen waited patiently for their marriage books, they started making plans for their second ceremony, which they hoped would feature friends and family. They wanted to have it at Ellen's church in Shanghai, the place she felt saved her life, and for Matt's family to fly in from the States. Unfortunately, they would later find out that Matt's dad, John, was unable to fly to China due to restrictions from his job, and Ellen's church was undergoing months long, major renovations, making it impossible to host a wedding there. So they ultimately decided it was best to wait until they moved to America.

For now, they accepted their marriage books and made plans for the future.

They planned a honeymoon in Malaysia in April of the coming year. After that, they would stay in Guangzhou only as long as it was required, which was at least one year, before Ellen could apply for her visa. If all went according to plan, they would hold a wedding ceremony in the United States on their two-year anniversary, September 27, 2020, alongside Matt's family, as well as Chris, and Ellen's aunt and uncle, whom she hoped could fly in.

* * *

After the ceremony at the marriage registration office, Matt had two weeks before starting his new job, and there was a lot to do before then—namely, finding a place to live.

For the first ten days after the ceremony, Matt and Ellen stayed in a hotel suite, as a kind of mini-honeymoon in the city they would now call home. After that, Matt's employers had provided an additional ten day stay at a hotel near the business. This allowed Matt and Ellen to enjoy their first couple weeks as a married couple while also making quick work of jump-starting their new life in Guangzhou.

As they explored the city, they asked God not only for guidance, but reassurance. Matt's choice to forego the Wall Street English interview in Shanghai had caught them both by surprise. And even though they trusted that God had stirred the curiosity and boldness in Matt's heart, and led them to Guangzhou for a reason, they prayed that they'd find both comfort and confidence in that decision.

Compassionately, that assurance came almost immediately.

With plans to move to the US as soon as Ellen could get her visa—and with regulations in place that required them to live and work in Guangzhou for at least a year before Ellen could even apply—Matt and Ellen knew they were going to be in constant contact with the American embassy. In China, the US Embassy is located in Beijing. Thus, if Matt would have taken the job in Shanghai, they would have had to travel back and forth to Beijing. On average, that's a four-hour, $500 round-trip flight—per person. And with a modest income to begin with, this would have been all but impossible. However, in starting their research on the visa process in Guangzhou, they found that in support of the embassy, there are also four consulates, located in Guangzhou, Shanghai, Shenyang, and Wuhan. Among these, the only consulate to offer and administer visas is that in Guangzhou. This meant that everything they would need, any person they needed to speak to, and any paperwork they would need to pick up or submit, was close by, requiring little travel and almost zero expense. Matt and Ellen took this information as a comfort from God, both that this placement had purpose and that their faith had been rewarded.

Matthew 7:7–8 NLT says,

"Keep on asking, and you will receive what you ask for. Keep on seeking, and you will find. Keep on knocking, and the door will be opened to you. For everyone who asks, receives. Everyone who seeks, finds. And to everyone who knocks, the door will be opened."

Matt and Ellen had asked and God had answered, so now they knew to keep asking. In a new city, living in a new home, working at a new job, with new people, as they started this new life, they needed to keep asking, keep seeking, and keep knocking. They needed to find the doors God had for them and trust that He would open those they were meant to walk through.

Matt & Ellen: The Beginning of Married Life

As Matt started his job, he and Ellen settled into their new apartment in Guangzhou and adjusted to life as a married couple, which proved to be a learning curve. They practiced extra patience with one another, trying their best to find a rhythm and fill their respective roles in the relationship. But living under one roof sharpened the cultural differences of their upbringings and heightened the language barrier that, while not crippling, still prevailed. These struggles came in tandem with those anticipated in a new marriage and the compromises that needed to be made—like with finances.

Alongside monthly rent due for their apartment in Guangzhou, they had to pay rent on Ellen's apartment in Shanghai until her lease expired. Ellen was also still taking English classes and Matt had student loans in America entering repayment status. Many months, as they tried to make day-to-day ends meet in China, Matt had to find room (and funds) to transfer money from his Chinese bank account into his American bank account in order to make payment on the loans, adhering to strict due dates that could incur late fees if missed.

As a result, they tried to spend as little money as possible. They ate rice and vegetables for most meals and budgeted down to only the essentials. It was limiting, frustrating, and constantly nerve-wracking as they neared the end of month when the numbers weren't adding up, and it seemed they would have to choose between paying rent and buying food. But whenever they felt their backs up against the wall, and it seemed all hope was lost, God would provide.

One especially scary month, Matt received an unexpected bonus at work. Not for a superfluous amount, not for a meaningless amount, but for the exact difference he and Ellen needed to pay their bills and buy their groceries.

At that point, Matt and Ellen thought God wasn't just providing, he was showing off.

* * *

When it came to cooking, Matt and Ellen often found themselves in somewhat of a standoff—one they were not expecting. Food had been something they bonded over. It was a shared passion that had sparked one of their first conversations on Hello Talk. When Matt visited Ellen in Shanghai, they had toured the city's restaurants and experienced the food together. After they got married and began sharing meals at home, the differences in their palates were brought into greater focus, revealing not just opposing preferences, but notable boundaries.

Ellen was thrilled at the prospect of cooking for Matt. She wanted to provide for her husband, to introduce him to her favorite foods and share the recipes she'd learned growing up. While Matt was excited to enjoy his wife's cooking and learn more about her through food, he and his "American stomach" felt nervous about the ingredients he saw her bringing home from the farmer's market. They were things he'd never seen before, never even heard mentioned in his corner of the American food scene, like bitter melon—a vegetable common in Asian countries that is shaped like a cucumber but has bumpy skin like a gourd. Ellen had grown up eating bitter melon with tomato fried eggs, but Matt couldn't stand the taste. There was also dried sausage, kelp seaweed, and gizzards, not to mention fish. While a very common protein all over the world, Matt had never liked seafood. So when Ellen prepared fish, he would often cook himself rice or vegetables.

In their first year of marriage, food became a sticking point. A source of conflict that neither of them knew how to broach. Ellen felt like a failure, like she was unable to be a good wife, and Matt felt incredibly guilty for not being able to appreciate all of her efforts. They found themselves having the same conversations and disagreements, with Matt doing everything he could to express both gratitude and awe at her cooking, even when he knew he couldn't (or wouldn't) eat it, and Ellen trying to explain to him how much she wanted to make things that he could enjoy.

It was a small obstacle that, in time, taught them how to communicate. It forced them to tip toe into uncomfortable conversations and encouraged them to compromise. As a result, they sought out restaurants they both liked and meals they both enjoyed. They began to appreciate one another's likes and dislikes and found humor in their starkly different palates.

After buying cucumbers at the market one day, they got into a discussion on how they'd grown up eating them. Matt liked to add salt and chili powder, while Ellen liked to add sugar. Both seemed equally strange to the other, but both defined a part of their respective histories which had come together in the grandest of ways. And when they learned to appreciate this rather than fight it, food once again became a shared passion through which they could express themselves and get to know each other, rather than a conflict that divided them.

* * *

Along with getting to know the rhythms of one another, Matt and Ellen also had to adjust to their new lives. Living in a new city, with new responsibilities, new goals, and new plans for the future, they both had to find their own footing on the new paths they were walking.

Matt was living in an entirely different country (not to mention a different continent) with a myriad of unfamiliar social norms. Matt had prepared himself for crowds, traffic and social congestion. But the packed subways, flooded streets, and waves of passing people was still unexpected and, at times, overwhelming, compared with southern California.

Ellen was now responsible for a household. She had moved away from her aunt and uncle, the only loving family environment she'd ever known, and was now in a new city, where she didn't know anyone except Matt. She had also left her job at Lee, and agreed to stay home and take on the majority of the cooking, cleaning, and laundry, all while keeping up with her English classes.

Nerves were high and money was tight. They were young. Unfamiliarity and inexperience rippled through each and every day, but Matt and Ellen stuck by each other and leaned on God. They asked Him to show them the way forward, not only in the months and days ahead, but in every moment they felt lost or unsure. And even though some days were tough, looking back, Matt and Ellen think of those early months of their marriage fondly. For among the uncertainty, there was joy, discovery, and humor.

As a couple in Guangzhou, they stuck out.

Matt's American roots placed him in the minority of the population, making heads turn whenever they saw him. Often, when Matt and Ellen would walk to dinner or ride the subway, people made direct comments in English, using slang words and phrases presumed common in America, like "dude," "totally," and "what's up, dawg?" because of their use in movies and television. Matt took these in good humor and found it fun to respond in English. He loved seeing the delight on the faces of locals as they realized that they'd utilized the English phrases correctly.

Another thing that made Matt stand out from the crowd? His arm hair.

Standing on the subway, kids would point and giggle at the dark brown hair, as visible body hair in China is far less common than in America. A few times, young children would pull at the hair, fascinated by it, and when Matt would flinch, they'd run away in hysterical laughter.

In time, the feelings of worry and loneliness associated with their move were overshadowed by love, safety, and an overwhelming sense of home that they found in each other and in this place. While they didn't have plans to stay forever, they believed God had them there for a reason and would move them when the time was right.

[ABOVE: VIEW FROM GUANGZHOU APARTMENT]

[TOP RIGHT: ENTRANCE TO APARTMENT BUILDING]

[BOTTOM RIGHT: HOUSING COMMUNITY MARKET AT NIGHT]

In Guangzhou, Matt and Ellen lived in a gated community, but not one you might immediately associate the term with.

It was not a collection of houses set behind a gate, opened either with a remote, a code on a keypad, or a form of identification presented to a guard. It was actually more of a small city, where tenants not only lived, but shopped, worked, and sent their kids to school.

It was a large, square complex, with entrances at the front, back, and both sides. Thinking of it in long, rectangular thirds, the front section, just beyond the main entrance, was home to shops, restaurants, and alcohol and cigarette stands; the center section encapsulated the rental units available; and in the back section, behind the apartments, was a farmer's market where freshly caught seafood, live chickens, fruit, vegetables, and raw meat that hung on hooks from the ceiling were all available for purchase.

Recalling their first trip to the farmer's market, Ellen laughs as she describes Matt's pale, shocked expression as he watched a live chicken's neck being broken and its head cut off after a fellow patron requested poultry at the counter. Being accustomed to this, Ellen had not thought to warn him, but as his expression changed from curiosity to horror, she blithely realized his unfamiliarity with a market of this nature.

A side gate of the complex offered passage to the local elementary school, as well as a shortcut to the local subway station. On workdays, Ellen would walk Matt to the subway, ride with him to work, and then return home to do laundry, make preparations for dinner, and study her English lessons. She would then meet him back at the subway when he arrived home, so they could walk back to the house together, catching up on the day's events and settling into their evening.

On one walk to the subway station, Matt had a strange feeling. Looking around at the city, at the buildings, the streets, the kids running around and the people talking, he began to feel as though he'd been there before. Sure, he had been living there for a few months and had grown familiar with his surroundings and the routine he and Ellen had adopted, but it was more than that. There was a sense that he'd visited years before even though he knew that was impossible. There was something comforting about the city, something sentient.

A few nights later, as the sun was setting and the twilight hours brought the colors of the city to life, something awakened in Matt's memory. Suddenly he was right back on that mission trip in the Dominican Republic, sitting on the porch of the house he and his youth group were painting, noticing the pinks and greens of the buildings that seemed to define the city. He had sat there with a kind of yearning he did not yet understand. He had felt drawn to the city, as if he belonged there, and he had heard a whisper from God.

You will live in a place like this one day.

He hadn't known what that meant at the time. Or how it would even be possible. But now, as he walked hand in hand with his wife, in a city, a country, a life he never could have predicted, Matt felt firmly rooted in God's plans. And he felt confident that he was going in the direction God intended him to go.

While this was comforting, it also heightened the anxieties Matt was experiencing.

If I am where God wants me to be, he thought, *and I'm with who God intended for me, then why am I struggling so much?*

MATT & ELLEN: UNDER DISTRESS

"Humble yourselves, therefore, under God's mighty hand, that he may lift you up in due time. Cast all your anxiety on him because he cares for you. Be alert and of sober mind. Your enemy the devil prowls around like a roaring lion looking for someone to devour."

— *1 Peter 5:6–8*

Matt first started to experience anxiety when he was very young.

He didn't understand where it came from or why he was experiencing it, so he had trouble opening up to people or asking for help, which in turn left him very isolated and forced to grapple with it on his own.

Matt remembers times when he would feel so anxious that he found it difficult to eat in front of other people. He would sit silently, nervous and unable to speak, feeling paralyzed by a fear he couldn't identify or overcome.

As he grew up, this anxiety would flare up in different ways with varying side effects. Sometimes it would feel like "butterflies" in his stomach, other times it would erupt into full on nausea. Sometimes his brain would feel foggy, making it difficult for him to stay cognizant and present in what he was doing, and other times it formulated into a stutter that both frustrated and embarrassed him.

When he was preparing to move to China and start his new job in Guangzhou, he had a few moments where he wondered how this was all going to work. He loved Ellen and felt blessed to have found her. He was excited to start their life together in China and had no doubts or second thoughts about marrying her. But teaching? In a foreign country? In a room full of people that were all looking to him for guidance? How was that going to happen?

In the days and weeks leading up to the start of his job, he often sat down and prayed the same prayer: *Change me. Please, God, change me.*

Surely, Matt thought, God wouldn't send him into this role with the same anxieties he'd always had. There had to be a metamorphosis of some kind on the horizon. A rebirth. A metaphorical shedding of skin that would remove the parts of Matt that were anxious, quiet, and afraid. He felt those parts had held him back throughout his life, and he now worried they would cause him to fail. So, Matt prayed constantly, hoping each night that he'd wake up the next morning a new man, a confident man, a changed man. But every morning, he felt the same.

A few weeks into teaching, Matt's boss called him into his office, explaining that Matt needed to be more confident. He brought up other teachers as reference points, advising that he emulate their charisma and energy, to stand taller, speak louder, and be far less tentative and meek.

This only made Matt's anxiety worse.

Compounded with the frustration that he wasn't doing his best work—and the fact that it was being noticed by his superiors—he grew scared and ashamed—not to mention angry with himself and discouraged by God's seeming dismissal of his prayers. He felt like a failure, and worried that he would be unable to provide for Ellen as a husband.

So he put even more pressure on himself.

He tried to will himself to be different by constantly self-critiquing. He continued to ask—at times desperately—for God to change him, to make him different, to take away the parts of him that had weighed him down for as long as he could remember, and now made him ill-equipped to do a job that God had seemingly pushed him towards.

Unlike growing up, when Matt had been able to hide his anxiety from others, he now lived alongside a partner. His wife not only wanted but *needed* to understand what was going on. Ellen could tell something was wrong, but Matt wouldn't (and couldn't) tell her. He had never learned how to express his anxiety or how to ask for help, so as he began to spiral into worry and shame, Ellen stood on the outskirts, only able to see Matt turn more and more inward—more and more silent.

In the mornings, he wouldn't—and couldn't—eat, no matter what Ellen made. And in the evenings, after particularly bad days at work, Matt would lash out inexplicably, causing the two of them to fight and grow weary, unsure of how to move forward. Tension grew between them, adding shame to Matt's guilt and insecurity to Ellen's confusion. She feared Matt didn't love her anymore and worried what that meant for not only their marriage, but their lives.

Then one day, after months of trying to navigate his anxiety alone, Matt broke down in tears and told Ellen everything. He started from the very beginning, telling her things he'd never told anyone else, revealing the darkness and fear that existed in him and controlled him for as long as he could remember.

Afterward, they prayed about it together. They brought everything to God: Matt's anxiety, the cracks it had formed in their marriage, the questions they still had about God's plans for their lives, and how to navigate the everyday worries that felt paralyzing and scary. They began to pray every night, side by side, saying everything out loud so they could face it together.

Soon, Matt began to feel Jesus move in his life. A new confidence developed in Matt that allowed him to first improve and then thrive at work. In time, he was named employee of the month and became a teacher that was sought after by many students.

It's important to note Matt's anxiety didn't disappear. God didn't remove the fear in order to help Matt succeed. But in Matt's surrender of the fear and anxiety *to* God, he was able to place his focus *on* God instead of the fear, allowing God to walk him through that fear, and causing the fear to lose its power.

"An important lesson I've learned," Matt says, "is that sometimes God will allow things like anxiety, heartbreak, fear, and pain, and not remove the hindrances we find challenging—at times paralyzing. Instead, He will invite us to bring those things out into the light, to surrender them to Him, and lean on Him. And when we lean on Him, He will walk us through it."

MATT & ELLEN: PROVISION

"And my God will supply every need of yours according to his riches in glory in Christ Jesus."

— *Philippians 4:19 ESV*

Shortly after Matt and Ellen got married, Ellen's uncle, a Chinese medicine doctor, gave her Chinese herbs that are meant to encourage fertility—and they worked, perhaps better and faster than expected!

In June of 2019, a few months after their honeymoon in Malaysia, and nine months after they got married, Ellen found out she was pregnant. This was exciting and blessed news, but it was also going to complicate things. With the one-year anniversary of their move to Guangzhou approaching, Matt and Ellen were ready to start Ellen's visa process and move to the United States. Having a baby in tow would add an unexpected layer, but they didn't let it worry them too much.

"A baby!" they thought. How wonderful!

* * *

Ellen's first doctor appointment was at a public hospital where rules didn't allow Matt to go into the room with her for the ultrasound. So as he waited outside the room on a bench, pondering the upcoming adventures of fatherhood, Ellen lay on the table, listening as the ultrasound tech found not just one heartbeat, but two.

"TWO BABIES?!" Ellen said as she sat straight up. "What do you mean?!"

"Shut up," Matt said when Ellen walked out of the room. "You're messing with me."

With shock came delight mixed with fear and the slightest bit of joyous panic.

What are we going to do?! They thought.

It was a high-risk pregnancy, they were told, and Ellen would need another ultrasound in a matter of weeks.

"Unfortunately," the doctor said, "there are no openings available."

Wait, what?

The public hospital worked on a first come, first serve basis and priority was not given to urgency. So even though Ellen was considered high risk, she'd have to get in line for an appointment, just like everyone else.

This, they realized, would not work. With three lives hanging in the balance, Matt and Ellen knew they needed to seek out the best help possible.

After doing some research, they found that the local private hospital offered a kind of "package deal" that would allow Ellen to schedule all of her appointments up front, making it easy to stick to the required schedule to ensure both her and the babies' safety. Then, at the time of delivery, they would go to the public hospital, as it would be far less expensive.

The private hospital equated to something of a five star hotel. The staff was nice and accommodating, the doctors were present and knowledgeable, and the facilities were state of the art. The only problem was that the price of the package being offered was significantly above their price range.

In talking with the hospital attendant and expressing their financial concerns, she ran the numbers again, this time including a discount being offered in honor of the anniversary of the hospital. While grateful, Matt and Ellen looked at the new price and explained it still wouldn't be possible for them to afford. They thanked her, preparing to leave and go back to square one, when she held up her hand and again turned to her computer.

As she typed, the woman explained that once a year, each staff member is given a discount—a coupon of sorts that they usually save for friends and family. But in hearing Matt and Ellen's story and seeing the necessity of high quality care for Ellen, she wanted to give that discount to them.

As a reminder, it was June, meaning there was an entire six months left in the year, when anything could happen. She wasn't giving them the coupon out of convenience or because it was about to expire. This attendant felt a call, a push to give this blessing to Matt and Ellen, even though a friend or family member could have potentially used it, and even though she'd never met them before.

They thanked her profusely, unsure if there was a way to fully express how much her generosity would help them. For even though the price was still relatively steep, with both the hospital anniversary discount and the staff coupon, it was no longer unreachable. With God's hand so clearly on their lives, on this situation, and in the heart of this woman, they had faith He would continue to provide. So, even though they knew full well that they couldn't afford to pay the remainder of the cost by the listed due date, they signed the paperwork, and they put the rest in God's hands.

* * *

In the weeks after Matt and Ellen walked out of the private hospital, feeling both blessed by God's intervention and the nurse's generosity, they wondered how they were going to salvage the remaining funds due.

A year prior, Matt's great grandmother had passed away. So as Matt began his new life in China, and he and Ellen entered their first year of marriage, Matt's family was home in the United States, boxing up his great grandmother's things, and preparing to put her house on the market. In June of 2019, the same month Matt and Ellen found out they were pregnant, Matt's family got an offer on the house and agreed to sell it.

Three days before the final payment at the hospital was due, Matt's family was able to wire money from the United States to China.

With the funds cleared, Ellen made her first appointment at the private hospital. Matt was able to be in the room with her, so they were both able to meet the doctor who would be monitoring Ellen and the babies for the remainder of the pregnancy.

The doctor had just transferred to Guangzhou from Hong Kong, but was originally from west Africa, which is home to one of the highest percentage of twins in the world.[9] In fact, he explained to them, growing up there had inspired him to become a doctor specializing in twins and the associated high-risk pregnancies. So by all accounts, he was the best man for the job.

Ellen and Matt looked at one another in amazement.

There was truly no detail that God had forgotten. There was no worry, spoken or not, known or not, that He was not calming. God was inspiring a faith in them they didn't know was possible. That faith would not only benefit Matt and Ellen, but anyone who heard their story.

Matt & Ellen: Visa Quagmire

With the healthcare package secured for Ellen at the private hospital, she and Matt were able to relax—not fully, as they knew their lives were about to change forever, but it was one big worry taken off their plate. And thank goodness, because a whole new slew of worries was about to bubble to the surface.

Shortly after Matt and Ellen got married, they filed a petition for Ellen to get a visa so that they could move to the United States.

In the United States, there are two main categories of visas: immigrant visas (for those looking to move to the United States permanently) and nonimmigrant visas (for those only looking to visit the United States for a set period of time).[10] Both visas have many subcategories that indicate more specific reasons and circumstances for the visit or immigration to the United States.

Ellen would need a CR-1 immigration visa, which indicates she, a non-US citizen, had been married to a US citizen for less than two years and was looking to move to the United States permanently.[11]

Matt and Ellen initially went to the American Consulate in Guangzhou to file an I-130 (a Petition for an Alien Relative) which would allow Ellen to come to the United States and wait for the approval of her CR-1 Visa. But upon filing that request, the Consulate informed them that they were required to live and work in Guangzhou for at least a year before their petition would even be considered. However, if they did not want to wait, they could submit the same petition to a lockbox in Chicago, which they did. Unfortunately, they never received a reply.

So in June, with two babies on the way, acting as their own personal alarm clock, and the one-year anniversary of both their wedding and their resident status in Guangzhou approaching in September, they decided to refile a petition at their local American consulate. This time, an approval to start the process came within a week.

To begin, they were asked to do two things:

1. Send a letter to cancel their petition at the lockbox in Chicago.
2. Provide copies of the babies' birth certificates.

Since the babies weren't born yet, they submitted a copy of Ellen's most recent ultrasound, along with a copy of the cancellation letter and both were approved.

Then the hard part started.

* * *

For Ellen to get her visa, she needed to submit two documents: a police check (which is the equivalent of a background check) and a birth certificate—the latter of which she did not have.

Having been born at home, Ellen was never given a birth certificate, so she would need to get one from the local notarial office. Two months pregnant, Ellen went in with her family book, also known as a hukou, or household register, which stated her name, her parents' names, and her place and date of birth, but it was not accepted as valid documentation of her birth. What she would need, the notary told her, was either her parents' identification cards, their marriage book, which would have the births of their children documented, or a written statement from her parents that declared they were present at her birth and could verify the date.

This was impossible! Five years earlier, before Matt and Ellen had even met, Ellen's father had passed away after a long-fought battle with cancer.

Ellen had been in contact with her family while her father was sick and had sent money when they needed it. During that time, she'd been able to better get to know her father and appreciate who he was. She was able to see a different side of him, a kind side that she hadn't known growing up, and she was happy to help him in any way she could.

When he eventually passed away, her family buried him. While this seems like standard practice, burials have been discouraged in China since the 1950s, when Chinese communist leader Mao Zedong declared that bodies should be cremated in order to save land.[12] Since then, some provinces—including Guangdong, where her parents lived—made the practice of burial illegal.

Nonetheless, in keeping practice with both their Buddhist faith and the ancient Chinese tradition of "returning one to their roots" (aka their hometown) after death—which is believed to help one's soul move peacefully into the afterlife—Ellen's family buried her father. And since they did so illegally, they were not given a death certificate. To make matters even more complicated, Ellen's mother had burned all documentation and identification of her husband, including his medical records and their marriage book, in an effort to help him "pass easily," leaving essentially no trace of him. This meant that there was no physical evidence or paper trail, thus, there was no proof that he was dead.

So, Ellen's options were either to provide identification of her father (which was burned), present her parents' marriage book (which was burned), or obtain a written statement confirming her birth from both of her parents (one of whom was dead).

Matt and Ellen went to multiple government offices, the police department, and the city official in the hopes that someone could help them. But as soon as the process would start, the issue of the birth certificate and then the death certificate would arise, and they were turned away, with each official claiming they were unable or unwilling to help.

After trying and failing for weeks, Ellen decided to look up the notary office in her hometown as a last resort. Her father had lived and died in that city. He was a prominent member of the community and thus his absence—caused by his death—would not only be noticed but perhaps be public knowledge, giving someone the authority to help her.

An office clerk answered the phone and greeted Ellen with a patience and understanding she and Matt had yet to encounter. He listened to what she had to say, from start to finish, lending an ear that seemed to be influenced by a force greater than her determination, and he told her what she needed to do. They talked at length about the steps she would need to take and who she would need to talk to, and he offered her continued support along the way.

But doors—both literal and figurative—kept being closed. Ellen once again grew discouraged. She reached out to the man one more time, dejected and desperate for any final suggestions.

The man grew quiet, considering her situation, and then did the unimaginable. He told Ellen that he would write and notarize a birth certificate for her. Having heard her story and seen her fight to overcome insurmountable obstacles throughout this process, he put both his job and, arguably, his life on the line. He drafted the document, allowing her sister (who still lived in Ellen's hometown) to cosign it and pick it up. She then mailed it to Matt and Ellen and they submitted it with the rest of their paperwork to the American consulate.

Matt & Ellen: Arrivals

By this time, Ellen was rounding out her third trimester. While she'd had a smooth, albeit stressful pregnancy, she and Matt were trying to get everything in place so they could leave China for the United States as soon as her visa came through.

But as the problems with her birth certificate came to a miraculous conclusion, the world took a turn for the worse. In December of 2019, a series of patients began checking into hospitals in Wuhan, China, 600 miles away, complaining of flu-like symptoms. As those cases began to multiply, seemingly by the day, rumors began to circulate wide and fast. Those who spoke out were silenced and often punished, leaving most people in a state of confusion, wondering what to believe, and doing their best to pretend like nothing was happening.

On January 3, 2020, China officially reported to the World Health Organization an outbreak of a virus similar to that which caused the 2002–2003 SARS epidemic.[13]

On January 9, Matt's mom, Karen, arrived in China to help them prepare for the arrival of the babies and to help them move to the United States. While Ellen was due February 8, most twin pregnancies are delivered at about 36 weeks, so Karen came early to help.

Throughout her pregnancy, Ellen had been getting ultrasounds every two weeks to ensure the health of her and the babies. But in her last trimester, the doctor had begun doing weekly ultrasounds, then multiple per week, then daily.

As cases of COVID began to surge, especially as people gathered all over the country to celebrate Lunar New Year, which began January 25, Ellen, Matt, and Karen waited, trusting God even in the throes of what was becoming true chaos. They prayed over Ellen, over the babies, and they asked for grace.

On January 16, Ellen's visa came through.

On January 22, Ellen had a C-section and gave birth to twin boys, Jeremy David Perrone and Jonathan Jayden Perrone.

Three miracles occurred, back to back to back.

Jeremy had been the name Matt and Ellen had picked the moment they discovered Ellen was pregnant. Before she'd gone in for her initial ultrasound, they'd had one girl name and one boy name written down, ready to commit to either one—though knowing they'd have to be patient to find out.

[THE TWIN BOYS]

Since 1994, sex screening had been illegal in China, due to the overarching preference for sons.[14] Over the years, it had become increasingly common for couples to have abortions if they were told they were having a girl, especially because of the one child rule put into place in 1980. Thus, sex screening or "gender reveal," which is commonly celebrated in western culture, was made illegal.

When Ellen walked out of her first ultrasound, fresh with the news of there being two babies on the way, she and Matt realized they wouldn't need just two names picked out, they'd need *four*.

After the boys were born, they held them in their arms, amazed, overwhelmed, and grateful beyond measure. Their names were special and picked with a purpose they hoped would follow them the rest of their lives.

Jeremy means "appointed by God." If you break that down further, appointed can be defined as "decided on beforehand" or "chosen for a particular job."

Habakkuk 2:3 says, "For the revelation awaits an appointed time; it speaks of the end and will not prove false. Though it lingers, wait for it; it will certainly come and will not delay."

In the Contemporary English Version of the Bible, this is translated to: "At the time I have decided, my words will come true. You can trust what I say about the future. It may take a long time, but keep on waiting—it will happen!"

Jeremy was the culmination of so many plans the Lord had placed in Ellen and Matt's lives. He wasn't a random combination of cells, he was wonderfully and purposefully made, planned by God long before Matt and Ellen could have ever imagined. Thus, his middle name, David, which means "beloved" or "dearly loved," acts as a promise to care for him, and to be grateful for the blessing God bestowed upon them with his birth.

Jonathan means "God has given" or "gift from God."

James 1:17 says, "Every good and perfect gift is from above, coming down from the Father of the heavenly lights, who does not change like shifting shadows."

God had remained faithful. As Matt and Ellen faced obstacles in their separate lives, and then in married life, God was always there. His hand was on their lives and His mercy was unfailing and unchanging. His light was constant through all of the dark—and would remain so going forward—and Jonathan was a testament to that shepherding.

His middle name, Jayden, means "God has heard," thus Jonathan Jayden together means God has given, God has heard. And indeed, He had.

Jonathan and Jeremy were born at 5 pounds 5 ounces and 4 pounds 13 ounces, respectively. Both were able to breathe on their own, and neither was required to go to the NICU. Alongside Ellen, they were all able to go home within a few days.

With Ellen's visa cleared, the only thing left to do was wait until the babies were old enough to fly—the doctor recommended about eight weeks. But on January 30, the World Health Organization (WHO) declared the COVID-19 outbreak a global emergency, and on January 31, the United States issued a nationwide travel ban from China for non-US citizens.

Lockdowns began to take effect nationwide. Matt and Ellen frantically began searching for flights, hopeful to leave China in March. Flights were being cancelled left and right. Three times Matt and Ellen were notified that the flight they booked to the United States had been grounded. With two newborns, a country in turmoil, and the world spiraling into panic, Matt, Karen, and Ellen clung steadfast to their faith, believing God would find a way. They packed up their belongings. They broke the lease on their apartment. Matt quit his job. But with each passing day, their window to leave China was closing, and as cases began to surge worldwide, it seemed to become more and more impossible.

MATT & ELLEN:
AT THE GATE

O Lord my God, you have performed many wonders
for us.

Your plans for us are too numerous to list.

You have no equal.

If I tried to recite all your wonderful deeds,

I would never come to the end of them.

— Psalm 40:5 NLT

In a typical video game, there is a moment near the
end of a level, or perhaps at the end of the game, when the
cheery background music becomes intense and fast paced.
The colors on the screen become dark and gritty; the
health level of the player blinks low, and the character on
the screen pants in exhaustion. Meanwhile, an enemy will
take shape, stepping forward into the center of the screen,
armed with weapons unknown. The floor might begin to
shake, and a barbed wire fence might appear, creating a
kind of arena you can't escape from unless you emerge
victorious. All odds are against you. Then the clock starts
ticking, the music gets louder, and the battle begins.

This is how Matt, Ellen, and Karen felt as they made their way through the airport with the twins on March 3, 2020.

Standing at the security checkpoint at the Shenyang Taoxian International Airport—they sensed this was their last chance. This flight was their final opportunity to get to the United States. But the TSA agent wouldn't let them pass. She insisted that the frozen breast milk in their carry-on bags be tested for explosives.

At first, Matt and Ellen argued, explaining that the breast milk had been cleared by TSA on their initial connecting flight from Guangzhou to Shenyang. But as the terminal grew quiet, and the full flight boarded its final passengers, they began to beg. They didn't need the bottles, they told her. Confiscate them. Throw them away. Anything that would let them pass and allow them to make this flight. Their luggage was on that plane. Their future was on that plane. But the doors were preparing to close.

The time on the clock was ticking, ticking, ticking, and the metaphorical music was loud. Each member of the Perrone family stood, trying to fight this final fight, but they all showed signs of exhaustion.

The babies were fussing. They were tired and hungry, frustrated by the way these travel plans had thrown off their routine. Ellen held one of the babies on her hip, her body still healing from the delivery and her energy level low from breastfeeding both children for the last two months. Karen was limping, unaware she had a torn meniscus, and that pushing through the pain as they hurried through the airport had caused her hip to partially dislocate. Matt was sweating, anxious to get on the plane, and nervous that symptoms from his three-day bout with food poisoning would be interpreted as COVID-19, and prevent him from leaving the country with his family.

They had nothing left. No home to go back to. No additional flight they could board. No other strategy other than to trust God. They begged the security guard to let them pass. They threw the frozen breast milk in the trash, and offered to throw away anything and everything else she might have an issue with in order to get on that plane.

The clock ticked down from five.

A voice came over the intercom and yelled, "Final boarding call!"

Four.

The once loud and crowded terminal was now silent and ominous.

Three.

Matt and Karen pointed to their bags, to the breast milk in the trash, to the babies.

Two.

"Please!" Ellen said. "Please!"

One.

The video game screen went black and the music cut out.

Then the gate rose.

The security guard let them pass, and they sprinted to the gate. Ellen, with Jeremy on her hip, handed her ticket to the flight attendant, and Karen and Matt, who was holding Jonathan, followed suit. They took their seats, lay their heads back, and let out a collective sigh.

They had made it.

But they weren't quite done yet.

Across the Pacific, another gate awaited. One last and final obstacle.

[DREADED SECURITY GATE TO ENTER THE
BOARDING AREA IN SHENYANG AIRPORT]

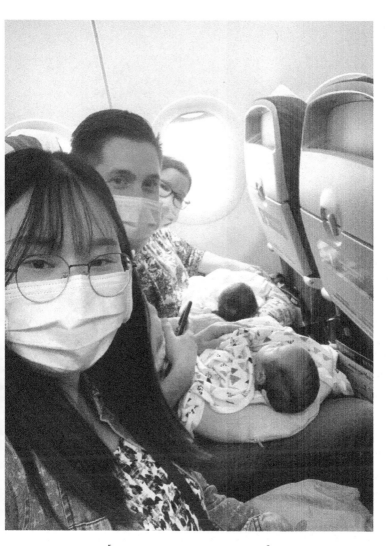

[ON THE PLANE TO AMERICA]

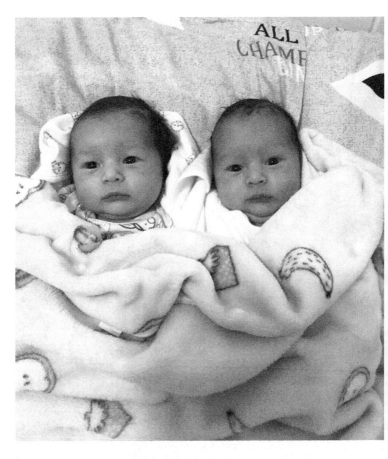

[THE TWINS BUNDLED UP
FOR THE LONG RIDE]

Matt & Ellen: Pieces into Place

For 15 hours, as the babies mostly slept, Matt and Ellen tried their best to prepare, talking it through to calm the nerves. It would be reminiscent of the first time Matt flew to China to meet Ellen, when he stepped into a bathroom to wash his face, his stomach full of butterflies and nerves, knowing his life was about to change. This time it would be Ellen making her way through immigration as Matt waited impatiently on the other side.

Though Ellen had her visa, she was still required to go through an interview with a customs agent who would give her final clearance upon arrival into the United States. She'd heard it was an intense process, and she was nervous something could go wrong. Ellen worried about her English, about whether she'd be able to answer the questions accurately and correctly, or to fully express the magnitude of what awaited her and her family on the other side of the doors.

Every single piece that had needed to fall into place to get them to the United States, to get Ellen in front of a customs agent to do this final interview, had fallen together in perfect timing. As she waited, she prayed God could come through for her one more time.

Just then, the babies started to get fussy. Matt and Karen planned to hold the twins while Ellen went in to be interviewed, but when the babies started crying, they wondered what to do. A nearby security guard heard them talking and suggested that Ellen take a baby with her into the interview room, as it might make the process go faster. So, Ellen took Jeremy and stepped into a side room and nursed him as she waited for her name to be called.

When she was finished, Ellen was told a woman was looking for her, and she again grew nervous. But when she presented herself to the woman, holding Jeremy on her hip, the woman simply handed Ellen her passport and said she could go.

There were no questions. There was no interview. The woman just let her go.

Just like the girl working at Ellen's store gave up her Saturdays so Ellen could finish her baptism classes; just like the woman who translated Matt's passport in under an hour on the day of their wedding; just like the man who drafted Ellen a birth certificate despite the utter lack of required documentation: God had always been there for her, had always come through, and now here He was again.

Ellen thanked the woman and turned toward the double doors. The very last set that separated her from her future, from the life she and Matt dreamed of in America. She had made it. *They* had made it. Against every single odd, they were home.

She pushed through the doors and smiled brightly at Matt. The same smile she'd given him the first time she saw him, before she could have ever imagined the journey they were set to take, and the blessings God would give them. Then Matt, Ellen, Karen, Jeremy and Jonathan, made their way out of the airport into the cool California air.

Outside, Matt's father sat inside a party bus he'd rented to accommodate not only Matt, Ellen, Karen, and the two babies, but all of the luggage they had in tow from China.

On their drive home, they stopped at In-N-Out, a tradition in Matt's family any time they returned from travel out of California. He was excited to introduce this local chain to Ellen, and to watch as she got her first taste of American od. Much to Matt's relief, Ellen nodded in agreement when e expressed how much better it was than McDonald's, one f the only American fast-food chains found in China while ey were there.

But what she found even more remarkable than the ood, even more meaningful than this moment of experiencing her first Perrone family tradition, was the Bible erse she found printed on the bottom of her soft drink up: John 3:16.

John 3:16 states, "For God so loved the world that he ave his one and only Son, that whoever believes in him hall not perish but have eternal life."

Hailed as arguably the most important passage in the ible, she now held this verse in her hand, printed on a red nd white cup, in America, with her husband, two sons, and ew in-laws.

She had a new family, a new life, and an unfailing faith hat had led her through darkness, conquered countless bstacles, and defied every odd. Every puzzle piece of her fe had a purpose, and God had put them all together.

EPILOGUE

If this were a video game or a movie, this would be the happy ending. Credits would roll, triumphant music would play, and applause would echo off the walls. All the questions would have been answered, all the battles fought, all the plot holes filled, and all the worries calmed. People would leave the theater, thrilled that the characters of Matt and Ellen lived on in infinite bliss, without a care in the world.

But these are not characters, this is not a work of fiction, and this is not the end of their story—not even close. Matt and Ellen consider themselves lucky, unbelievably so, that they have seen the hand of God work so clearly in their favor, giving them faith to last multiple lifetimes. But this does not eradicate further struggle, upcoming doubt, or impending obstacles. They will still face trials and they will forever be given new reasons to lean on God. Their faith will always be tested, just like everyone else's, and it will be a daily choice to trust God and His plans for them.

Christian singer Riley Clemmons' song "When Nothing Hurts" asks of God, "Make me desperate for You, even when nothing hurts."

Throughout Matt and Ellen's journey, they met many obstacles that they didn't see a way around. Whether it be health issues, financial difficulties, anxiety, visa approval, or mass flight cancellations, Matt and Ellen were continually put in situations where there was nothing left they could do. While these struggles were not easy to go through, they provided opportunities for them to turn to God.

We might not all experience the same challenges Matt and Ellen faced, but we will all go through times of trouble, doubt, chaos and darkness, where we too can find opportunities to turn to God. But it is easy to forget that the same opportunities exist when we feel happy, content, satisfied and calm. We forget that faith is not just leaning on God in the hard times, but actively seeking Him in the good times.

Philippians 4:6–7 (NLT) says, "Don't worry about anything; instead, pray about everything. Tell God what you need, and thank him for all he has done."

Pray about *everything*. Everything good, everything bad, and thank him for *all* that he has done. This is a challenge of faith that Matt and Ellen, and you and I will face every single day.

So as the miracles of this story wash over you, and you consider the what-ifs in your own story that reveal the proof of God's influence in your life, challenge yourself to put God first. Openly and actively trust Him, even on days that don't feel particularly challenging or desperate. Reach out to Him, even when you aren't lost or confused or broken.

For Jesus said, "My Father is always working, and so am I" (John 5:17 NLT).

He is always working. For you. For me. On good days and bad days. In big moments and small ones.

Be patient. Take heart that God has a plan for you and that it is all coming together in perfect timing. And what's more, find purpose in the fact that in living out the plans He has for you, you are acting as crucial puzzle pieces of countless other plans. You might be exactly the person someone needs on a given day. You might be someone's miracle without even knowing it.

When we trust God, we do more than strengthen our faith; we do more than point ourselves in the right direction and calm the fears that threaten our very foundation. When we trust God, both when things are easy and when they're hard, and we allow God's faithfulness to pull us through darkness that we feel we can't escape from, we do more than find peace. When we trust God with our greatest fears, biggest dreams and our most daunting what-ifs, it is not only our lives that are changed. When we trust God, we can change the world.

REFERENCES

1. In 1979, in an effort to control overpopulation, China began enforcing the one child rule—a policy that stayed in effect until 2016, when the restriction was changed to two children per couple. See https://www.open.edu/openlearn/education/brief-introduction-the-chinese-education-system.
2. Tania Branigan, "China's Great Gender Crisis," Guardian, November 2, 2011, https://www.theguardian.com/world/2011/nov/02/chinas-great-gender-crisis.
3. "What Is Pharmaceutical Chemistry?" University of Florida, https://pharmchem.cop.ufl.edu/about/articles/what-is-pharmaceutical-chemistry/.
4. Qian Kan, "A Brief Introduction into the Chinese Education System," Open Learn, August 30, 2019, https://www.open.edu/openlearn/education/brief-introduction-the-chinese-education-system.
5. Dezan Shira et al., "China Visas Explained," China Briefing, October 16, 2019, https://www.china-briefing.com/news/china-visas-explained/.
6. "China Work Visa," VisaRite, https://www.visarite.com/china_work_visa.htm.
7. Shirley Li, "China's National Day/Golden Week," China Educational Tours, https://www.chinaeducationaltours.com/guide/china-national-day.htm.
8. Antoine Boquen, "China's Hukou System Explained," New Horizons, June 28, 2021, https://nhglobalpartners.com/the-chinese-hukou-system-explained/.
9. "The Land of Twins," BBC World Service, June 7, 2021, https://www.bbc.co.uk/worldservice/people/highlights/010607_twins.shtml.

10. "U.S. Visas," U.S. Department of State, https://travel.state.gov/content/travel/en/us-visas.html.

11. "What Is The Difference Between IR1 Visa and CR1 Visa?" Pride Immigration, February 7, 2022, https://www.prideimmigration.com/what-is-the-difference-between-ir1-visa-and-cr1-visa/.

12. Frank Sieren, "Burying Tradition in China's Anhui Province," DW, May 7, 2014, https://www.dw.com/en/burying-tradition-in-chinas-anhui-province/a-17760549.

13. "Timeline: China's COVID-19 Outbreak and Lockdown of Wuhan," AP News, January 22, 2021, https://apnews.com/article/pandemics-wuhan-china-coronavirus-pandemic-e6147ec0ff88affb99c811149424239d.

14. Reuters, "New Chinese Law Prohibits Sex-Screening of Fetuses," New York Times, November 15, 1994, https://www.nytimes.com/1994/11/15/world/new-chinese-law-prohibits-sex-screening-of-fetuses.html.

BIBLE VERSES

Each verse has been noted with its referenced translation.

1. Esther 4:14 (paraphrased from ESV)
2. Habakkuk 2:3 (NIV & CEV)
3. James 1:17 (NIV)
4. Jeremiah 29:11 (NIV)
5. John 3:16 (NIV)
6. John 5:17 (NLT)
7. Matthew 7:7–8 (NLT)
8. 1 Peter 5:6–8 (NIV)
9. Philippians 4:19 (ESV)
10. Proverbs 3:5–6 (NIV & *The Message*)
11. Psalm 40:5 (NLT)
12. Psalm 119:105 (KJV)
13. Philippians 4:6–7 (NLT)

Made in the USA
Las Vegas, NV
19 April 2023

70808799R00063